MW01204851

Weeds to Ash

Portraits of Suffering, Seeking, Overcoming, and Love

Simeon Jubilee Griffin

Thanks friend,

DEDICATION

For those that are able to see past the typos and recognize their beating heart within my own,

For my parents – to them my endless love,

And as always for Big Love Now.

CONTENTS

Music

I saw a shirt that said:
Un
f█ the world.

And I think I can get behind that.

SUFFERING

Cigarettes 1.

I thought my depression was what made me relatable

So I held on

But also because it was familiar.

However,

When I grew older,

My depression is what isolated me

Because as we get older the better we are at concealing.

It is only in that period of adolescence that we are allowed to feel

Confused, dark, doomed, afraid

But when we grow up

It is mandatory

That we feel

Brave, unique, directed

And not depressed

So my depression left me alone.

Cigarettes 2.

In my isolation

I had my own work to do

I sat in dark rooms

And shared "feelings"

Or rather things I didn't understand

To someone I either didn't know

Or who I was afraid to disappoint.

I would say

I don't understand why

I want to kill myself every Thursday

When the churches are closed

And I'm so very sober now

So sober it's upsetting.

They didn't tell me it'd be like this

No, they just ushered me off

In my rehabilitation

They didn't tell me it would be like this

And I suppose that is why no one ever wants to get
sober,

Because I am now forced to feel all of life

And not just its pleasure.

Overrun

My mind is a temple
In which I seek sanctuary,
Yet it has been overrun
By demons and pain.

Anti Depression

There are twenty pills on my dresser to fight anxiety
There are twenty pink packed chemicals there to
remind me that I am broken
There are twenty little circles that no one seems to
understand and whom everyone has an opinion of
There are twenty reminders of the sleepless nights
spent with razor blades and heavy breathing
There are twenty bitter pills talking freely of how easy
it is to die
I'm not sure why life is like that
I'm not sure why people don't understand
I'm not sure why this state of being is so easily
dismissed
Maybe because it is in the mind
Maybe because our thoughts change all the time
But it's not just in the mind
But rather it interlocks itself through every joint and
seam and pulverizes my body
There are twenty little soldiers hopeful today will be
okay

ER

I can hear the sirens before I get to the house
The red and blue flash high over the rooftops
I park the car and sit for a minute
It feels just like every time
It's probably the same paramedics too
Even in my memories I can still see the open
mouthed screams

Musings on a Grey Heart

I get up this morning, thinking I will work very hard
These shackles from past stories keep me caged like
an animal
I fight fire with fire, burn bright in spite of life's
desire
To put my little flame out.
These chains wrapped around my back are clues to
my lack of freedom
This free doom, this perpetual lack of room
Sirens and flashing lights
I'm afraid of missing out or getting left behind
I look at distance and track it on the map and wonder
If this move will kill me too
I don't stay put because I am afraid to
I don't stay put
I am a furnace and a engine, burning as bright as the
sun
I am an eagle on a mission to find God's only son.
Has my only mission become trying not to lose the
Jupiter within my heart?
Has self preservation become my only intention?
Has the protection of that that is dearest to me
become my sole obsession?
I look upon crowded streets and fail to see my face in
the people I meet
And wonder if there is love present in this heart of
mine
Or
If perhaps there is only fear.

Mm.health

They saw open the top of the head
To pour either
A. Puzzle pieces
or
B. Acid
Down inside.
They meant for me the puzzle pieces, but I was a wild
child and the acid splashed inside.
Now I must spend the remainder of my years
Trying to piece together puzzle pieces
That no longer fit

Mirrors

On some days
I don't look once at my reflection
I cringe when I hear what my voice
Actually sounds like
Or observe my quirky mannerisms
And it seems
Every ounce of laughter
Is directed directly at me

Things no More

I won't come home anymore
When momma dies
There will be a roof over our heads
But no home in our hearts
I think the fire place went cold
When momma died
The kitchen was never used again
No more sweet smelling bacon and eggs
And no brushing tears away
When momma dies
Sleepless nights will stay sleepless
No sweet lullabies
Or trust in Jesus
When momma dies
The family will no longer gather
And there will be no birthday cards
Coming in the mail
Signed dad&mom in momma's hand writin'

We'll all gather graveside
Throw our flowers
Say our goodbyes
And miss her forever
When momma dies

and some more nightmares

Wintered weather
Fall'd & Ball'd

Night terrors each time I sleep
Venom, Venom, Venom
Snakes shed their skin
Sirens cry from the water beneath my bed
I pray to God
But even the heavens have turned their heads

Martha Olive Orange

The past comes in like a disease
It's tireless sleep
Opens doors to our homes
& forces us on the street
Tells us we'll be left alone
& swears it never leaves
The past comes in
The past comes in
The past is my disease

Cousin

I pictured his blue eyes
His warm smile
How he always had something to ask you
About what made you
Distinctly
You
His tone
Of
Voice
And how he's been missing
For over a month now

- September 2016

Sadness

Was I given an extra scoop?
A double dip serving?
And then my cone fell to the ground
On top of all that?

My soul died with me.

My soul died with me,
But my soul had never really lived,
Because I spent my time in
Conformity,
Appealing, pleasing, and living in
What was expected of me
And what made me special,
What lied deep with my soul,
Died
When I said yes, yes, yes
Far too many times.

I'm so sorry

I feel like a
Cactus
As of late
Every word hate
Every action
Pain.
I offer my condolences
I offer my apologies
But I feel like I am
Leaving wounds
In my wake
When I always meant these hands for healing.

To care for

Everything I have ever written has been a cry for help and either I have no voice, the world has no ears, or there are far too many of us.

Permanence

There is a promise I have made
That I am not sure I can keep
The weight of the world upon
These hollow, hollow shoulders
They ask me how my thoughts are
They ask me if I'm planning again
They don't know that I am lying
That I say I am good because
Their worrying does no good
That I tell them what they want
To hear because they provided
The help I did not need
The evil held at bay by white knuckles
They crack though
They bleed though
They grow weak and I am worried
That someday I will not be able
To repel all my demons and
They will swallow me whole
Then all the words I have ever
Tried to write
Tried to speak will be as
Those other authors who
Took their own lives
Trying to write of love and hope.
These words are mostly for me
Trying to believe in the power of
The love and hope I speak of, but
This thing follows me everywhere I go
Torturous.

Innocent

Really
Really
Really
Trying not to
But I've always looked
For reasons
Something to point to
As to
Why I am feeling angst
And their unsuspecting eyes
Various shades of hair
Fluctuating voices
And soft tears
Are my focus
Even though I wish to kiss those tears away
From every face
Including my own
But I can only touch the cold
Hard reflection of the mirror

1,000

My time was filled
With a thousand reasons
Why
My night was filled with
Sleepless
Sighs
A worried
Mind
Tired
All the time

love

Funny how the things they say can stick with us
And the things they prey can pierce us.

Black

I've always worn my heart on my sleeves
That's why I have the saddest eyes you have
Ever seen.

Dreaming of Phone Calls

I hear the
Nervousness
In your voice
Like you are
Scared to tell
Me something

violins

I spent time in the desert
I named it my soul
Because I was so familiar
With this barren wasteland
I thought I was home

~depression

Bandstandquicksand

I don't like revising
I don't like rewriting
Because that would mean
I would have to read
What I wrote
And I don't want to see
What could possibly
Come from these hands

feels like sometimes

Nothing
Here is nothing
Signed with a pen
From myself
A friend
Here is nothing
All I have to give

SEEKING

More poems on forgiveness

It's this act
That's the hardest to get over
The hill the just keeps growing and growing
It circles in the mind for days
It'll lessen
And it will appear to leave
But rush in like a hurricane
Reminding that it has the power
It needs to leave
Because there is so much more important things
More valuable things
But this one thing
Blocks the view of beauty
And suffocates the living
It's important to move past
The mole hills made into mountains
Because at the top
Is the smallest of views
Only revealing all the things
That were missed

Aging

I am imprisoned by city blocks, starched shirts, and ridged collars.

I WANT A HOME MADE FROM EVERGREENS THAT WILL BURN AS BRIGHT AS THE SUN.

I am bound by cropped haircuts, gas prices, and shitty beer that I drink even though I don't want to.

I NEED DIRT BENEATH MY NAILS AND HAIR ON MY FEET. I NEED SPRING WATERS TO BATHE IN AND JOIN THE SALMON IN THEIR SEEKING.

I am claustrophobic from the demands of others and the fear of saying no, so scared to come across as boring or worse yet, for who I truly am.

I WANT TO WALK NAKED IN THE FOREST, CLIMB TREES THAT HAVE NOT BEEN SCARRED BY CARELESS CIGARETTES TOSSED FROM WINDOWS BY MEN THAT CALL THEMSELVES HIPPIES, BUT HAVE NEVER ONCE CARED FOR MOTHER EARTH.

I am a mystic in a land that banned magic. A painter living in world where black fumes pollute the atmosphere raining ash down blotting out the color.

My soul is in a state of sickness that is curable if only I would care for myself. But the moon is almost full and I need to drink again.

Al(own)e

I love your writings and you have so many friends. I've seen movies so I know what that's like. The laughter, the applause. The friend who gets too drunk and says everything that everyone's been thinking, so you thank them.

I dance in my kitchen too. But alone, not in a sad way though. I don't mind being alone and I'm never really on my own. I dance in my kitchen so I can smile down at me. There isn't any worry then, about what the eyes might be seeing or the mind be thinking. I dance to Jimi and the Beatles, the Roots and the Who.

Wondering who I am

Who I am

I am

a.m.

And the alarm rings and sounds a new day to discover who that is.

A song

A song
a sound
a noise
a god
a voice

~Just before I fall to sleep

Seventeen

THE WORLD IS MINE
AND YOURS
HIS AND HERS

When I was 17
I was sneaking out of bedroom windows
Onto roofs to howl at the moon
I would squat, pipe in hand
Spark a flame and leave this dreary land
I would re-enter
Amber glow meeting my eyes
Shower, eye drops, cologne
Hide my lies and the red veins
Interlacing my eyes
A lot of showers when I was 17
Skin marked by the parch
And raisin lines
Soap would dribble and fall behind my ears
I had two friends
The first you've met, my pipe
The other my fears

Eyes that are asleep

I see that familiar shadow
The one that lies behind four years
Of sobriety
I see the familiar shadow
Standing behind me
I keep my face on the sun
Yet, I see that familiar shadow
Lurking
As if it had never left

- *Relapse*
- *October 29th, 2012*

and on

i know what you mean
there are a million
traps in my mind
snares in my heart
alarms in my head
that keep me restless
and my nights sleepless

Spaces

There is a space between my dresser
And the wall
A space between my bed
That the pillow slips
Through
There is a space
Between my
Front teeth
One I worry about
A space between
Between
Between
That my lips meet
There is a space between
Where I stopped writing
Letters to my future wife
And now
There is a space between
Myself and confidence
And I suppose
That is where the problem lies

Stories

In my mind
It makes waves,
On the page
It is as flat
As a lake
With no ripples
And an ocean with no
Rage

Dreams & B.F.F.s

I've seen every last one of them die
Snakes wrap around necks
And I'm just a child
Having never seen a dead body
I scream,
But my voice is caught
My voice is caught
Who stole my voice
And why am I here?

BRPI:.

Poor boy soup
Don't ignore the bluesy stoop
Where children stop their playing
Stare aware at building blocks
Swaying atop these roof-e-tops
They don't smoke cigarettes
Yet
Because they haven't seen enough t.v.
Won't do coke and filter it
Until
They are at least seventeen
At most seventeen
But perhaps
Not before then.
Cut baggies
Maybe before then
But no powder
Power
In nostrils and sinus
Till moon is purple
And they've lost all the wisest

Alcohol

Burning
Fire
Belly
Melted face
I feel I can be my truest self
I just keep saying the wrong things

This House

Everything is so fleeting and temporary,
Yet we will spend our whole lives
Trying to make it permanent.

Stages

Hello, hello, goodbye.
Hello, hello, goodbye.
Hello, (hell)o, goodbye.

Cold Showers

I've always been able to think of reasons to die
This morning I thought
When the cold hit
My skin fizzled and pop
Shrivelled and rot
I've always found reasons to stay
Still finding reasons to live

White Light

Now my minds clouded
Reverse
Reverse
Look away
I'll stare at the sun until
I can see it all
Said
I'll stare at the sun until I can see it all.

There is a sunbeam at the end of the hall.

There is a sunbeam at the end of the hall.
It calls, it calls,
But when I approach the curtain draws.

writing

It hasn't felt like me
Freeing these letters
Love is present,
But whose skin am I in?

- Nobody cares

soft

Someone says
Carelessly
YOU AREN'T GOOD AT LOVING YOURSELF
And even if you were
Even if you are
You start seeing all the reasons why
You're not
And begin to wonder
What's the point
If you are always going to be
This broken

Writing again

Even if it is the worst thing you have ever read,
My heart will still beat
And pump red.

Confused

Mixed messages
Meaning
I missed the message
Somewhere back where
You left it

My skin, I live in.

My mind isn't organized,
Is yours?
I can't find what I'm looking for
Nor do I know what's in there.
It is a portrait of me
Layers upon layers
Of something
Maybe flesh and blood
Emotions, dreams, and fears
Growing deeper and deeper
All too much
To go through
And know every inch of
It piles to teetering
Some things valued
Some things not
Fall off
And I continue to grow
With or without them.

Perhaps I should inspect these wounds and see if
there is anything I would like to keep, maybe even
rewrite and revise my dreams.

The Wall

I feel this wall whenever I sit to write
I feel this charm, it is a charm
A weight pushing me back against the wall
Demanding I get up from my seat
Demanding I step back from the keys
I feel this wall
Pushing me away from my dream
And in this moment
That is all I have to write about

seeing stars

a star fell from the sky
Before it was time
if only love could have
Held it there
what would it take
Another day, another year
i wish i could bridge
Every gap
between
Every ounce of pain
and all people
Could finally
Stop hurting

Not True Pt. !

I am not a whitewashed tomb
I am a broken man fully bruised
See my wounds? See my wounds?
I am shame. I am regret.
Sitting in hands that are blessed.
I attest. I detest.
Constantly vexed by the hex within my chest.
Beating my breast
I arrested my best.
I am a jungle of snakes and lies
I am mask of love but it is a disguise.
I am vipers in Eve's garden
And God has been trying to get
The snake out ever since

Compare me to what?

Would I be more confident if I was the Harvard grad?
My degree holding such promise and prestige?
Would I feel perhaps more lovable if I was out in the
broad world?
Living the "abundant" life rather than here right now?
Would I feel like a better catch if I was not myself,
but someone else?

Would I feel more beautiful with a smaller frame?
And look up at the man I love rather than meet him
eye to eye?
Would I feel more prosperous if I had graduated "on
time?"
Would I feel more at home if I never had to come
home?
Would he love me more if I wasn't so wild?

Vultures of Culture

I keep seeing it, hearing it, feeling it
        These great birds circling overhead
(spst...you inspire me)
They flap their great feathered wings
Remnants of blood and guts hang from their jowls
        Do birds have jowls?
        Men do.
They smoke their silver cigars and stack their shillings until
the golden house they made disintegrates
I'm pro money, anti insanity, pro living, anti establishment,
and still awaiting these tears to fall
   Out to clouds and sky and to move the heart of God
I've never felt like less of a man than...
        Right then, right now
     •   **murder men for money**
        •   lambs for wealth
     •   borrow children for cash
     •   mattresses filled with coin
BUT IT ALL STARTS TO RUST
BUT IT ALL TURNS TO DUST
Why choose to become a monster to chase after things
that only take away? When has money ever given me
anything more than a craving for more? I must live. I must
survive. But a house on a hill will not make me come alive
inside. The job will not validate me. The sleek car will not
make me thin. The woman, the ring, the mass amounts of
money will not buy any form of security.
I'll spend my time living this free gift of life
rather
Than pursuing something that someone else has
promised will buy me life
AND I HOPE I CAN HOLD TRUE TO MY
CONVICTIONS
AND NOT WAIT TO LIVE ONCE I'VE AMASSED
MY WEALTH

BECAUSE IF I WAIT TO LIVE ONCE I HAVE
MONEY
I WILL HAVE LIVED SEEING NOTHING BUT
FANTASY
AND DIE VERY VERY, VERY MUCH ALONE

...

my mind is a catastrophic mess
of thoughts that disappear with time

slowly living

breath is life
And life is death
Because at that very first breath
We begin to know death

letters painting no pictures

My diary is filled with
Half cracked ideas
And unfinished stories
It's full of thoughts I don't

Understand

And letters that could be
Profound
If only they weren't lacking in
Photographs

Comments on Life / Little Lives

My slowly sorrow siren song
Unwinding like the break of dawn
Here in the briefest of blasts
Just before it's solely gone

This too is for me

I don't need to be the most interesting man alive
I have no need to travel every place
Learn every tongue and know every face
The world excites me only because
It offers up keys and helps open doors
So I can further explore me.

~Perhaps Selfish

Fall's Call

Bummer bummer bummer
I called back Summer
She said she was busy hold the line please

OVERCOMING

Heart & Mouth.

If we remember we can stand
We'll see we are taller than before

Moonshine

Death isn't a scary thing
It's just something that happens
Loosing people is the scary thing
Because it's just something that happens

Moonshine fades
My luxurious grave
Bedside stories
Of how we regret everything

When I am old with age
Regret will not even be a shade
Held within my eyes
Within my face
Only pride in the smiles
And how lovely I behaved

When the wizard plays his games

I've been wondering what I should do
When I graduate
Which path I would choose
When I graduate
Whose would be whose when dollars are few
When I graduate
All I know is I'll marry you
When I graduate

~Cool

Absent Abyss

I said goodbye to whomever
In a letter
I burned it
And tossed the ash
In the river
I made amends to so-and-so
By looking myself in the mirror
Acknowledging these scars
And promising I'd
No longer live in fear
I made peace with my past
By forgetting my past
Meaning I forgave my past
Meaning I'm free at last

Trying

Stilted
Gets hard to write when you walk on cinders
Gets hard to think when the floor is cold
And you roll over on the stone
Tucking newspaper into your shirt
To stay warm
But we all want to be the creative types

Dreams Again

The stars cried out
In their sleep
Afraid, afraid, afraid,
Lonely, sad

But the moon was
Right there
Said do you see
This light
You can never be
Alone
I reflect
A million suns
I reflect
A million yous

Comparisons

Trace the snake's
Curvature
See the tail
Lace lines in the air
White lines of wide eyed stares
See the demons
Spill steam from my ears
My mind is an engine
And this is the first time
I've decided to set
Foot in the control
Room
I've decided not to crash
And burn
Because I will live while I am
Alive

Why I cringe/Why I cry

Every time I've been at my most vulnerable
I've been hurt
And I hope you can understand that…

For Myself

I go down alley ways and abandoned streets
Digging in garbage looking for something to eat
I chose this life, it did not choose me
My whole life I've wanted to sail by my own flag
It took me twenty years to build the boat
And another four to plant the mast
Now I pull the rope and it ripples in the breeze
I brush off death because there are sights to see
Whether painful or joy filled there are days to seize
And I will not play nice nor stay safely docked
On this shore of disease

tumblr

I miss writing letters to you
It's the clearest way I can communicate
I miss reading your words
Such a picture of the mind
I read your words today
Tumbled
I wanted to read something
I hadn't yet
And it was notes to other boys
Ones you had fallen in love with
It was notes of struggle
Of the deepest pain
Notes of insecurity
And finding security in love's name
I read that thing
About LAWLZ NO
Same height or shorter
And I get to thinking about what your thoughts are
Right this minute
And every second since March
I wonder what notes
Tumbled through there
Which ones you wouldn't want me to read
We all need space to place
The thoughts that litter our head
We all need a spot to pin
The I LOVE YOUS
And things left unsaid
At the end of this one
From me to you
 I LOVE YOUS
Is all I've ever said.

Feeling Tired

I'm trying to muster up the strength
That I will need for the day.
I am trying to muster up the patience
That I will need for these people.
I am trying to stretch my lips
Into a smile
And welcome each beating heart
As if it were my own,
But my lips turn downwards
And my eyes flicker and grow
Heavy
And I stop trying.
I cease striving.
I sit back
And sip a coffee
Praying that I will be enough for this world
And almost start to cry
As I remember that I don't have to.

Today is about gratitude

And then I remembered.

But enough about me

When I first asked if I could kiss you
There was a surging of fear in my gut
But I did it anyways
Because you are worth
Every bloody wound that turns to
A harden scar
And at the end of life my skin
Will be as armour
And my heart as soft as melted gold

Scrolling

Sometimes I wish I could talk to myself when I was
younger
Tell that sleeping child, wild and wild
That the pain in his tummy was only hunger
And the numbing of his heart was only wonder
Just as a man goes deaf from the roar of thunder
If I could see myself at seventeen
I'd say avoid the drama queens
And trying to be cool with the fiends
Go to the principal's office more
And chat with the dean
Dream more and constantly wonder about things
unseen
I'd say question everything
Build your own foundation
Write songs on probation
And only sleep for procrastination
Every hour awake and aware
Stare at the sun till it's no longer there
Bear your heart and let your sleeves no longer care
Meaning you don't have wear your emotions there
Meaning people don't drive you
Shake hands with God and man
And wrap yourself in your own love
Till you can stand or fly or all the above
I promised I'd fight for you
And I would love you fiercely
That is why I am on my knees
Crying out to this ever present
God, please, please, and please
A whole land washed with disease
A lifetime of pain and death

In between
The air is cold and the sky so bleak
The lies stand as the tallest trees
And truth is needles hidden
Within the weeds
A whisper in the wind
As I listen to what you need
I promised I'd fight for you
And here I am bleeding upon my knees

White Bath Towels

When I was a little boy
They would tell me I should be an actor
They said I could do whatever I wanted
Be anyone
So dream big, They'd say

When I was older
I told a man
I wanted to be an actor
We sat in white towels
In a gym sauna
He said, Join a local theatre
Perform in a couple plays
And be done with that
Because you can't make a living
That way

Why do they wait till we're older to break us?
Why do they justify shattering dreams with this thing
called REALITY?
If reality has no room for dreamers, do not beacon
children to dream.
If dreams can change reality,
Please.
Oh please.
Shut the ██ up about my dreams.

I see old men who have gone years with sleepless
nights
Because they have accepted an acceptable reality
That has forgotten how to dream.
I WANT TO REMEMBER.

Neural Pathways vs. Reality

I've been writing music these days
No, I've been dying in my rage
Lying to myself
Saying I'm no longer in a cage
Paying wage after wage
To keep my age
But remain a slave
I am silly meter
And silly rhyme
I am easy words
That come fast
And stay with time
I am not Whitman
Not immortal
And very contained
Between my boots and my hat
I'm lost to greatness
And bound by fate
To be left behind
When Jesus calls us to his gates

Rather
I am the breath of life
The sun lives within my mind
And I am the rays
Burning quickly
Yet bringing warmth
Cold bodies welcome me
Even if I am such a vapour
I am the breath of God
I am beauty made

In his image
Bountiful
Endless
Not bound by the limits of my body
But alive in the limitlessness
Of my spirit
I will be dancing at heaven's gates
Forever loved
This is all our fates

Lay it down

I refuse to let the better
Get the best of me

I refuse to allow culture
And doctrine to prevent me
From loving myself any less
Loving others any less

I AM A SINNER, BOUND TO SIN AGAIN.

There is no excuses there
No loopholes or trying to escape
From something
Not justifying or perhaps justifying
But I have determined that I will raise
Myself learning to love better
Even if I make a lifetime of mistakes
I want to love you better
Even if I fail you countless-ly
I want to raise children with confidence
Not ones that are so afraid of doing wrong
They live in a constant state of self-doubt
And are never able to choose
Nor make a decision on their own
Because I know those types of children
There's one that lives in me
And it is now up to me to raise him

Love

Family

Perfection

Is not

The picture I can paint

But my family is healthy

Because we have all agreed

To work on ourselves

Independently

Together

-From them, I've received more encouragement than I could ever ask for

-I have more love in my heart for the four of them and all of their extensions than I could possibly begin to describe

-my mother, my father, my brothers ~ *I love you all*

Love is

I am thankful you are there to listen
When I don't know what to say.

This little square

Let us pause
Right here in this square
And hold one another
There are a hundred reasons
To harbor hate
But to every one
There is an infinite amount
To express love
Let us hold tight to eternity
And not grab hold of fleeting bitterness
Love is eternal
It is in you
And it is in me
So hold me
And when we step out from this square
Let us remember

the day after thanksgiving

I love my body
Not because of the right curves
Or the perfect weight
Or just the right amount of muscle

But rather
I love my body because
It carries love
And kindness
And hope

And all of those are reasons to love
And all of those are enough for me

Big

Since I started seeing you,
I've enjoyed going back and reading what I've written

It isn't something I laid out
And left
Like a stamp I pasted
And sent away

But rather it became a reminder
Of how capable I am
Of loving well

And to me
That's beautiful

I told you once

I have a bible for you
It contains all the reasons why
I'll say, "I do."
All the dreams and futures
That contain me and you.

I have a bible for you
A manuscript explaining
Why our love is true.

read this.

Of course there's repetition
Moments of boredom
Mundane
Days and weeks that
Feel all too much the same
Of course that should be expected
Love is finding the beauty
In a moment
You have lived a thousand times
Love is seeing new in your partner's smile
Love is not letting the same day overtake you
But rather pouring color in a world gone grey.

Everything

I saw the moon in your eyes
Old, young, and new
Ever waning/waxing
Crescent
And full

blessing

I can count the stars
And place your name among them
And you will last far longer
Than Earth ever would

Signed,

god

Press3d

I took a break from breathing
And spent my time kissing you.

tw1l1ght

I have never felt more at home
Then being tangled up
In the warmth we
Create together

They only need to be washed away.

I kissed you a hundred times in the night
And a hundred more when we woke
I loved you in every dream
And forever when we rose

nightmares are not big.

I saw that you were dreaming
Clouded dreams
So I pressed my head against yours
And brought my world to yours
We were in a city
Europe
or something
The buildings were tall enough
That the sun couldn't kiss us
So we tore the buildings down
Planted seeds and trees
We built up mountains
And paved paths with our feet
We kept the sun as close as our love
And sent the clouds on their way

Even Though

Oh
Even though my heart pulls out from my chest
I will still push you forward
Even though a part of me goes missing when you do
I'll still usher you out the door with your bags all
packed
Even though I long for you and you are water to my
soul
I'll still wave to you as the airplanes send you up and
away
And I'll be waiting for your sweet return and yes, I'll
still be living.

It's easy loving you.

I am here holding you
Making promises
I will stay true to
Gripping your waist
Through pain
Through joy
And everything in between
I fear losing you
I fear getting left behind
You moving on, you finding someone else
Leaving me, losing me
I fear the death of love
Losing the most profound
Thing that has ever entered
My life
This is what makes love hard
It is not love
But the demon of fear
This demon takes me through loops
Tunnels, caves, scenario after scenario
That are not my own
It takes me along the scenic route of pain
Yet here I am
In spite of it all
In spite of it all
Here I am
Still gripping your waist
Winkles line our face
New time
New space
There I was in youth
And here I am in old age

promises in bathrooms

the world is caving in outside
it is moving like ants do
swarming, swirling, whirling
but let's be present here
and let me speak truth
i hold your head
and grip you waist
i hold it tight
to let you know there is
a force here
to let you know
i mean what i say
i tell you about the kids
we will have
how i will fight for them
i talk about our demons
how i will fight them
i talk about the past
how it couldn't matter less
how it means nothing
holds no power
nor influence over my love
for you
tears are streaming
but i will not let myself get
choked by them
i hold your waist tighter
and say
that i will fight for you
like no man ever has
i will be there for you
like no one else

ever could
i will be you warrior
i will love you
and please you
and serve you
and be a present constant
in your life
i will fall to my knees and pray
and rise
and do battle with anything
and everything
that would ever choose
to set foot in our way
i will kiss your lips
and touch you so tenderly
as if i was approaching fire
my love will burn and beat
bright within my chest
it will be so fierce
and so strong
there will never
ever
be a second of doubt
in your mind
in your heart
that i am for you
i am with you
i have chosen you
and i choose you
you are my equal
my lover
my very best friend
my lovely muse
my lovely muse

keep writing poems
on my heart
i will always share
how much i love you
and i will continue
to find a way to describe
that
to you

~*a long one*

dreaming with you

We pass out of the canvas of sleep
Your breathing is erratic, panicked
I grip you face and place my lips
Where you say you love me
It's only a dream, whispered
That was months ago

Last night, I sensed you tense
I was fast asleep
You grabbing at your body
Breathing short and shallow
I lift you up from the pillow
And cradle you in my arms
That soft spot
The one meant for you
I put my hand on your head
Much like you did for me
That first night
We stay like this until
We pass through the canvas of sleep
You say thank you for pulling me
Out of that
I say thank you for being so
Welcome in my arms

Well Rested

My mind is a fire
Burning with ideas
Your heart is the paper
Where I pen every kiss
Your skin is the lullaby
That sends me off to sleep
And our dreams
Are shared together
Because love
Is always free

UP

Vast differences
Masked penmanship
Hidden messages
In secret letters
Tied to string
Attached to balloons
Sailing towards
Your heart
Hoping to
Make room

Telephone Timing

May I hold you hopeful?
Kiss your tears with tenderness
And you kiss mine
Let us turn sorrow to salvation
And whisper the wind away

Homecoming Queen

I could sleep
But instead
I go back to my room
Play your music
Read your blog
And look at pictures of us
So I can listen to your sounds
And know you more

story of man

I sing songs while I'm driving
Ones I make up to keep out the quiet
I cry tears* when I think of Psalms
And hope that love interlaces these willing palms

*almost

To nothing

I have yet to find something to compare you with
I could look upon a diamond or a rose
But I do not wish to wrap you around my finger
And hold you there and you are continuously
blooming
I could hold you up against the light or perhaps
A fireplace, but you are brighter than the sun
And provide much warmth
I could compare you to other women or what I am
told
Beauty is, but I decided a long time ago I'd
Determine what beauty is and I would know it
When I see it and now I do
I have yet to find something to compare you with
And I am grateful something so rare and one of a
kind
As you would be so in love with me

Awaiting

I searched google and couldn't find you
I went through my contacts and couldn't
Contact you
I found residue
In my photographs and messages
But I wanted human body and form
So I went to your window
And tapped until you awoke
A little frightened
But my lips tended to yours

Elfish

I wanted to sit and write today
And make something beautiful.
So I simply thought of you.

Mad Inside Jokes

I turn to the cross
To movies
To magic
I see your love slipping through the seams
It's a secret type of love
One that enters our dialogue and lives well within us
It is a secret type of love
One that is meant for everyone
But will not demand the spotlight

A start

I woke up early

The day after I was born.

Monday Pt. I of VII

The days are sailing by
Literally sailing by
It's as though we are on a ship
&
We are racing with time
Using its momentum and our own
To leave these days behind

If I'm not careful
I'll find myself wishing for Saturday
No, not Saturday as in the end of the week
But Saturday as in the moments I spend with you

That can happen on a Monday morning
A Tuesday evening
A phone call after work on Wednesday
&
A late night on Thursday

I'll wake up with sleep in my eyes on Friday
I'll realize today is the day I have to say goodbye
I'll bolt upright and wrap my arms around you
And think please don't go, please don't go, stay here
I'll kiss you on the lips
I'll kiss you on the lips once again
And I'll say,
I'M EXCITED FOR YOU
And I am.
I'll say,
GOOD LUCK TO YOU. MARVELS AWAIT
And mean it.
I'll say,

I CANNOT WAIT TO SEE YOU AGAIN AND I
WON'T WISH AWAY TIME FOR MORE
SATURDAYS
And I'll really try not to.

But we all know Saturdays were meant for lovers

Tuesday Pt. II of VII

Last night was haunted by waking dreams
And things in my room
I could flip on the light and they would leave
But I would be admitting they were there
To begin with
I kept it dark and my silhouette hung in the mirror
Like a ghostly haunting
My mind dived in spiritual realms
And I started wondering how
Why
What did I do to cause this
Are the demons that haunt us always around
Because of our actions
Or do they maybe just pass through
And is the fear I felt
Simply the vast loneliness that
Encapsulates them
Is that why they are so scary?
Because we recognize the emptiness
The complete isolation
They perpetually wander through?
Are we afraid because we know what we
Would do when faced with that kind of
Loneliness?
The desperate measures
The thoughts
The lashing out
I think I was so afraid, because I feared
They would lash out at me
Take me captive and do
Something
But they would have no need to do

Such a thing
Nor could they
Because I'm bathed in the sun
And I can see in the night
And those orbs of loneliness
Are just stars that have gone dark

Wednesday Pt. III of VII

Last night was filled with major alarm
False alarm
And two extra hours of sleep

Last night was spent in comforting arms
A lover's arms
And warmth wrapping around me

Last night was conversation unhindered by harm
Unravelling past harms
And a well spring of the deepest deep

Thursday Pt. IV of VII

I don't have the answers
To all the tough questions
Sometimes I feel like what comes from my mouth is a
wellspring of wisdom
Sometimes I don't
I try to offer my two cents
To be the leader that I know I'm created to be
In this I know there are things I can do better
Things I can stop doing

Sometimes I wake up sad and have no idea why
Sometimes I repeat a phrase over and over to myself
until I believe it
But often those phrases are run unintentional in the
back of my mind
And often they are self-deprecating
I'm trying to be a worthwhile human being
I see so much grace for other people
I see men who have started wars
And parents and lovers who have caused immense
pain
But I've always felt there is forgiveness for them
It doesn't matter what they've done
There is still love for them
That they still are good and whole and healed
I struggle to feel the same about myself
I see my mistakes
Feel the weight
Know the pain I've caused
And I cannot think that I am good
I cannot think that I am loved
Because look at the power behind these fists

The death held within these lips
Look how I could cripple you
Destroy you
Rip your heart out
Look how I've crippled myself
Destroyed me
Ripped my own heart out
And I think there cannot be love for me
Look at what I've done

Yet I continue to hear this sweet song
Call out to me from the driest of deserts
It says come child, come
I say no
I say you do not want me to come
You will not love me when you see my face
You could not love me when you see the blood upon
my hands
The song is sweet
It says sh sh child
Hear my voice
Hear my voice
I am every love you have ever desired
I am what you are looking for
Even here within this desert
Come, let me wet your tongue before you die of thirst
I shake my head
Shake it fiercely
I say no
You do not want to water me
Let me die out here without a stream
That's why I have found my way into this desert
So I may die of thirst
So I may rid myself of stepping on anymore toes

So I can never never never hurt the ones I love again
Let me die.
Yet the song continues
And in the coils of death
I cry out
Why have you forsaken me?
I cry out
Do you no longer love me?
Is what you sung to me as a child all so very much a
lie?
It all feels quiet
It all feels still
I lay my head against the sand
My lips continue to break open and bleed
Until there is no blood left to pump through this
lonesome heart
That's when I begin to hear the song again
It says I never left
I call to you each day
I wrap you in my arms when you're fast asleep
shivering at night
I am the whisper that speaks to you late in the night
That-
Speak to me in words I can understand I scream into
the wind
Sand coats the inside of my mouth and it all becomes
so very still
A river forms and grass begins to grow
I am led to the waters
And slowly lowered in
The cool water gently
Kisses my troubled skin
I am submerged
And stay until I can breathe again

I lie in the grass and fall fast asleep
THE DESERT SAND BURNS THROUGH MY
SKIN
AND THE SUN BLISTERS MY BACK
I jolt upright
The grass is still beneath me
The river still moves beside me
I never left
I never will
…
I let out a brief sigh
And consider going back out into the desert
I can still see it
It's behind me
I don't feel that I belong here
And I feel like that will make it hard to stay
Even though this is all I've ever longed for

Friday Pt. V of VII

I think I'm going to do it
Write over the weekend that is
Get my fingers sticky with ink that is

I've been hearing a lot about hustle
Grinding, persistence
I know what I want, but I think the hardest part is
patience
I had class last night
And people said their majors and what they would do
I was the only one with a creative pursuit

The self doubt slips in
Because people start talking plan bs and safety
Like it's the safe thing to do
I start to question if this is what I want to do
If this is something I would love to do
To wake up every morning and write
And then I realize that's what I already do

Saturday Pt. VI of VII

Last night, it was 2:00am
I searched her blog as I always do
There was a new post

It was about us
Our love
Our future
Our present
Our past

We are getting married you know?
In one year, two years, three years, four
It doesn't really matter, because we will share our lives
together
Each year will pass and we will become something
new
There won't be sharp edges
Or old wounds
Because faults will be dulled in her love
And in mine

I could never be as [poetic] as I'd like to in describing
us
It's not a fairytale
It's two children who have decided to hold hands
forever
Even after
They find out there is no such thing as fairytales
It is teenagers with woes and angst
Who see themselves in the other
And realize they are welcome in each other
It is grownups who see life's responsibilities

Demands and dangers
And still choose to live like children
In the land of devils
But devils hide from children
Because they cannot come near purity

So my dear,
May I always love you with a full heart
You deserve it
May I wash your feet and remind you
At all times how exquisite you are
Because you deserve it
Let my words be endless in adoration and praise
That I have taken flight with this angel
You
You are a mixture of magic and majesty
A toss between grace and gorgeousness
You are holy and pure
Sanctified and righteous
And I will ever be at your side

There is no longer a need when the pieces have
aligned
Some day there will be a perfect poem
The right words
To express my love for you and my reception of your
love for me
And every day will be our wedding night
And I'll read these vows over and over again

Sunday Pt. VII of VII

END OF THE PROLOGUE.

Some goodbyes are harder than others
But with you, it's never goodbye.
It's always hello,
Because even when you leave
I'm always praying for more hellos.

Expectations

There are these things called expectations
The things I have been programmed to expect
Worse case scenario, heartache, and death
I have learned time and again that to have hope
Is the riskiest thing I can allow myself to do
Because as soon as I start to gain hope for marriage
I hear of another divorce again
As soon as I hope to find friends
I start losing them
As soon as I hope for a lover
It all starts to fall apart
Except with you.
You see
You are rewiring my brain
Because you are here
Breaking my expectation that you'd leave
I can feel hope creeping in
My first instinct is to crush it
Before it can crush me
But you keep loving me
You keep holding me
And kissing me late into the night
You don't meet my expectations
You are breaking them
Turning them to dust
And building a platform for real love
To stand upon

[you]

It's those tiny moments
The warm hand on my arm
It's those tiny moments
The briefest movements
Smallest motions
It's when you put your hand on my leg
And start spelling my name
I can't stand it, because it tickles
So I push your hand off
But your weight, your body, your lips
Your smile, your love
I'm so thankful that is something
That is in my life
I'm not sure how to say this
Even though tickling is tickling and
I have to fight your hand off my leg
I am so thankful that hand is there
Does that make sense?
Tickling isn't pleasant
But it is pleasant because you are present
Does that make more sense?
There is pain, sure
There are valleys
And sandstorms
But they are all reminders that you
You are present
You are present
There are great joys
Mountain peaks
There are moments when
I am closer to you than I've
Ever been with another human being

You know me in ways no one else does
And I know you in ways that no one else does
These all bring me immense pleasure
Because they are a reminder
That you are present
You are present
What a present
I LOVE YOU
I love you because you are
And that is enough
I love you for being
And that is enough

When I say, "I love you," what I really mean is...

I mean I want to hold you in my arms completely and forever.

When I say you, I mean you. You completely as you are now.

When I say now, I mean neither the past nor the future.

Though I do hope we have a future, even more than that

I want an eternity with you right here in this now.

Start off the day at least trying to describe it

I try to find the right inspiration
In order to channel this
This, this big present love
But all my words are futile
Attempts to describe something
Indescribable

Yet, I can still feel your tongue circling mine
When I close my eyes

And I saw the stars bleed tonight
Dripping colors on our canvas
They aligned like the lines in our palms
Like freckles and good night kisses

ESSAYS

to my friends with the loneliness

August 29th, 2016

I heard you were crying tears at night. So was I. I heard you get seasick and forget how beautiful you are, sometimes I do too. Isn't it hard when we feel so uncomfortable in our own skin? I have friends that make my skin feel more comfortable. It's like I was suppose to wear them around or walk hand in hand with them, but the truth is I like the way their skin feels against mine. It reminds me that my skin is warm, my skin is soft, but I don't always see it that way. I just notice their warmth, their love, and the smoothness of their persona. They are impeccable and I am… Well, I am me.

You know when people say marvellous compliments, confirmation, and words of affection and adoration and all you want to do is say, "No, no, not me, but you!" I know you know what I'm talking about, because we share some of the same friends and from their lips is a wellspring of life, of inclusion to remove us from our seclusion. It gives us wings to soar and fly above the things that appear as mountains, but are only little hills. But what if we had wings already and those friends were just reminding us that they were there? I think that is more of the truth, because I've never had a friend give me a pair of wings, but I've always been able to fly with those that blow wind into my sails.

For those of us that are experiencing loss or the distance between friends seem far too great, for those of us who sit in now silent rooms once filled with laughter and who feel the silence bearing down, you still have wings. You still have wings and you were always meant to fly.

A GOOD FRIEND IS NOT THE WINGS UPON YOUR BACK, BUT THE WIND UPON SAILS. A BEST FRIEND IS NOT THE THINGS IN WHICH YOU LACK, BUT THE HEART WITHIN YOURSELVES.

How to deal with heartache, heart break, and distance

There comes a point in all of our lives where a sweet heart leaves, families move, friends grow up and grow out, and sometimes we are the ones to leave.

So what to do when the heart is distraught, when loved ones are miles upon miles away or when they are right next door, but unavailable and the deep onset of loneliness creeps in. I haven't the answers entirely. I think the better man is born within us all and we have yet to see or fully know him.

Her beauty is so captivating, how or why would I ever take time to know or grow my own soul?

My family is a blanket of warmth, why would I ever brave the cold?

So here's the bullshit first:

1. Breathe, breathe, eat, sleep, rest
2. Spend time with new places, faces, and friends
3. Read, read your life away, let fiction drizzle from your mouth and knowledge fill your ears
4. Write, write your heart out, pen to the page, the rage, the bliss, the misses, the fidgets, and the sickness. Pour it all out and breathe.
5. Dream and be and know that this is your life. Alone or with someone, no person nor thing can make you whole. So dream a life for yourself and allow the people to fall into place.

Now the truth. The only thing that matters:

Thank God for humanity. Love big. Love always.
And love everyone. The feeling of being with family,
a lover, a friend, a child are not unique to one time or
situation, nor a single person. Love is cultivated,
grown, and replicated. It is in the sun through the
trees, God's light to us. It is in the flicker through the
leaves from the campfire at night, our light to God.
Love is in the birds that sing in the morning, the
white light, the breeze through the window. But that
is the bliss. Let's now experience tragedy, because
love is there too. It is in the single breath you are able
to breathe into your lungs, just to allow your heart to
break a little more. It's in the scars and the body that
heals so quickly when the razor blade tells lies, saying
it is the only way you are able to feel. Love is in the
skin and molecules, the blood vessels, the mind
racing, love is in your body, moving, healing, floating,
working, even when you cannot meet your gaze in
your own reflection, even when the words "I love
you" dare not whisper from your lips.

It's not the people, the places, the things we
experience. It's the love that penetrates and permeates
all things and what we choose to do with it, how we
choose to receive it, how we choose to give it.

**Distance can make the heart grow stronger. It
can make our hearts grow fonder, because now
instead of five feet, there are thousands of miles
of love between you and me.**

The Art of Being Naked

I saw an old woman today who'd been widowed thirty years.

She still wore her wedding ring along with a warm smile.

She said she was filled with a plethora of, "It feels like yesterdays" and "I remember whens."

I was bold and reckless and asked, "Would he not want you to move on?"

She laughed. And laughed.

"But I have," she replied, "We all do."

I've moved on to days without him.

But I've moved on to days where I'm closer to him.

I can't outrun him so I don't try. There is a tombstone that marks where and when his body left the earth, but it is just a point on the map."

She rested her chin on her hand and looked thoughtfully off into space. Her eyes old and sad. The oxygen hooked up under her nose whining and whistling away.

"He still speaks to me, you know? And when the sun just peaks up over the horizon and the dew is still fresh in the air, I can still feel his lips against mine.

I spent years with no one. Just myself, my bootstraps and a backpack. I can do on my own. I can do lonely. But I would still dream about what he'd be like and what our lives would be like. Then I lived it and we lived it well."

She laughs again.

"We were nude more than we were clothed. That's the secret."

She winks.

"It's not sex. Don't be fooled child. Sex is sex is sex. But nakedness, that's vulnerability. You can have sex without that. But you can't be naked and not have that. We'd swim and dance and run through the rain. We were children at heart. We still are."

I smile. She's holding my hand now looking at me like she sees something I cannot.

"So you dreamed about it, then you lived it, now what?"

Her face brightens and she sits up like she has realized something of extreme importance.

"Now I get to remember it."

WEEDS TO ASH

For a Walt Whitman

Who didn't teach me to read or write

But gave me words I could fall in love with

And for you, dear reader

I hope you can fall in love with mine

Stories about Me

(Non-narcissistic)

(I believe)

(A secret)

(Of how I turned these weeds to ash)

[1]

Birth, bread, bread of life, and water

Convinced of my conception

Perpetuated but not prevented by contraception

So it begins and as quickly as it does it ends

A breath and dust in the wind

My heart not existing and then beating with hot coals
or fire and then as cold as stone

So these sandy grains that spread so quickly in the
wind

Washed away through feeble finger tips

So how *should* I live, I mean how should *I* live, how
should I *live*

I suppose with roots dug deep, swaying with a wind,
but not faltering

Or perhaps pluck myself up and set foot as a
vagabond

My boots grow weary from the treading

But my heart is full

[2]

Lost to music and the great depression

My present obsession has turned to my present
frustration

Growing wearing with the whirl of reruns and
misguided episodes

Being called gay and fagot

Not because of a foot path I walk, but rather to
remind me that I am hated

Children of the corn wear horns and expose me like
porn

Pulling me limb from limb to use as timber for hellish
fires

I just wanted to fit in

Scoffing and mocking and bullies and fiends

Teaching me how to loathe my self, my flesh, my
bones

The education of self loathing

Elementary, middle school then on to high school

Graduating at the top of my class

Scars lace the insides of my arms

Horizontal as not to pass, pass, pass away

Simply to feel something fresh

Tear soaked puddles attempting to liberate my heart
from its camouflage of blistering hurt

The fiery red wounds rub raw on the identity of my
peers

My mouth seals shut or becomes vibrant in
boisterous violence

I smoke cigarettes so my insides can look like my
outsides and they both could feel the same

Remembrance of the first violation of my virgin lungs

Black rolled cigar

Lit with a match

To be coughed up in relentless rejection

Tears stream, thankfully I am alone

[3]

The fire of the sky alights the clouds with its embers

Remember when we were kids

And said the things we did

You thought we would just kid

But meant the things I said

I did, I did

When I asked if we could marry

*But your parents said you were destined to be with Prince
Harry*

We laughed, yet I felt confused

Because you were here with me and I wanted to stay here with you

But as I grew up, I realized that I, myself, am a Prince

And you are a queen

and perhaps YOU CAN RELATE

But it's not every day that I feel this way

In fact there are some where I feel like the village idiot

Pray they will pillage and plunder all things that are a hindrance from me

I find my self in the desert, in the ocean, or a forest

Where for once all things can be equal and we start again

[4]

Needles protrude from willing bodies

My destiny warns that life gets graphic for the next four or five years

Lungs fill with fumes, bath salts, and melting plastic

Not born asthmatic, but trying desperately to run out of breath

Eyes dilate, expanding and subtracting

Perceiving that I am actually seeing the world

The posters on my wall grow stale

Gods of rock and roll crinkle and tear and bow

Hanging there in solemn embrace

I try to about face my life 2,346 times

But I like my drink, my smoke

My purple syrup to drizzle over my pancakes

A breakfast for champions

My hands full of vitamins slowly dissolving on the
tongue

The bitter burn as I swallow my escape

I prefer these things to this reality

The horse tranquilizer carefully caught up and I
reached paralyses in ketamine

The rhythm of my body boosted by ecstasy

Fatal features in the light of the storm swirling

I swore, I swore, I would never

Methamphetamine

The mind collapses in on itself, my nose now filled
with snow and blow

Bumps of coke off key chains

My mind rings from the pain of sobriety

I sell my blood, plasma, and my seed to pay for

My dubs, laughter, and my weed

I steal birthday gifts, wallets, cash, check, cards, coin,
and rust

From family, friend, stranger, and enemy

To pay for escape, elation, and ecstasy

I lie and break trust like bones

The splinters and shards of white fly in all directions

Piercing flesh and heart and love and mind

I am a liar, a thief, a lover, a sinner

A cheat, a stealer, a feeler, and a killer

My person is fake, is phony, is lost, is lonely

Is blasphemous, but wants a god

Hates people, but wants friends

Loathes thyself, but wants to be loved

[5]

I am my own parent

My own lover

My own child

My own adventure

I am a product of my happiness

Not that I create the imbalance that goes about in my mind

Causing me to roll over and take the pink antidepressant on my nightstand table

But as my mind is whole

I am my own friend

My own author and storyteller

I am the greatest of actors and

I choose which performance to perform and for who

I decide where I leave the grave robbers and monkeys I have carried on my back

I decide when to cut out the bottom of my rucksack

Releasing the miles and piles of stone that do not
belong there

Yet, that I have placed anyways

I am my own hope

My direction

My muse

My peace

My journey

No one inhabits this body, this form, but me

No demon, no thing

No angel, but in best wishes perhaps a God

My dreams are my own

I decide whether or not to breathe life into them

Or allow them to wither and die

I choose whether or not to pick up the pencil or pen

Or what have you

The mic, the guitar, the instrument

The song, the voice, the dance

The brush, the can, the art

The trade, the talent, the career

I decide who I love and who I allow close

I protect myself

I set boundaries

I leap

I love

I hope

My fate

You will never make those decisions for me

Not because my ferocity deems it so

But because you will never inhabit this body

Just as I will never inhabit yours

So may we never allow another to chose our life, our
destinies for us

This is truly for ourselves to decide

[6]

Oh boredom, my simple acquaintance

A quiet nagging in my head

A prostitution of the things that must be done and those in which I desire

There is a moment when art does not pay your bills

And it must not be stripped naked and thrown into muddy streets to be pulled and prodded over

I do not create beauty to prosper

I prosper because of beauty, thus I create it

It has yet to line my pockets with gold

Yet I continue

Because I prosper in its beauty

The only reason I wish for gold lined pockets from my creation is simple

I only wish for more time

More time with my saw-dusted hands manipulating form

More time for ink riddled fingers to find structure

More time for my back to give way and break from
being hunched over the perils of the typewriter

It is as if I am at sea

Myself the captain

Striding among the lumber, bought and sold

Rotted and warped from sea and salt

I climb the mast and grip the sail

And will the wind and the rain to follow me

I lose sight of where I am

Awake on sea shore, sea shells, and lions

The sun breaks through the clouds and I see that you
and I

Are beautiful once more

[7]

I whittle weeds once more

The poetry and prose that comes from my lips, is as
sweet as yours

The cherry blossom, full in bloom

The roses and sweet alcoholic beverages, taking us
under their wings before we even realize

My back feels lighter and I stand more erect

My soul is wholesome and love, all the more blessed

With each touch, peak, or thought, my heart fills to
brimming over

Witness our quiet sound, the voice in our head

Follow us through the crowd, okay to be alone with
oneself

Is that not why we read?

Because we are okay to be alone?

Because we are in love with ourselves, or at least okay
with ourselves

Braved the isolation, to tell stories, read poetry in
caves, drink beers underage

& be with ourselves and those that love art

So if you are here, sitting, reading, you are among the
bravest.

DEAR READER

Dear Lover,

You've made it to the end. Was it a troublesome journey? A blissful one? Regardless, I am thankful you took the time to read my heart and attempt to understand me. I hope it offered some insight into your own heart as well, that would be the dream really.

Life is various, but there is always beauty in between the seams.

Sincerely,
Simeon Jubilee Griffin

ABOUT THE AUTHOR

Simeon Jubilee Griffin lives ███ ████████████ and
███████████████████████ loves Jesus
███████. He ████████ desires that
before he shares a name for God, he ████ shares the
name of love above all else. ██████
███████████████ he continues to believe in
the beauty of his dreams.